GOD IS
NO
ILLUSION

GOD IS
NO
ILLUSION

Meditations
on the End of Life

JOHN TULLY CARMODY

TRINITY PRESS INTERNATIONAL
Valley Forge, Pennsylvania

Trinity Press International, P.O. Box 851, Valley Forge, PA 19482-0851
Trinity Press International is a division of the Morehouse Publishing Group

Library of Congress Cataloging-in-Publication Data

Carmody, John, 1939-1995
    God is no illusion : meditations on the end of life / John Tully
Carmody.
        p. cm.
    ISBN 1-56338-188-5 (alk. paper)
    1. Terminally ill – Prayer-books and devotions – English.
2. Suffering – Religious aspects – Christianity. 3. Carmody, John,
1939- – Health. 4. Multiple myeloma – Religious aspects – Catholic
Church. 5. Death – Religious aspects – Catholic Church. 6. Catholic
Church – Prayer-books and devotions – English.   Title.
BX2373.S5C37 1997
242'.4–dc20   96-42947
                                                                   CIP

Printed in the United States of America

97   98   99   00   01   10   9   8   7   6   5   4   3   2   1

For
Alfred Corn
Paul Crowley, S.J.
Klaus Porzig, M.D.

CONTENTS

FOREWORD

I will not presume to tell you what you will learn from this book. I can only tell you what I am learning. For best results, *God Is No Illusion* should not be read; it should be prayed. Early in the morning as I try to "waste time with God" (Ignatius Loyola's description of prayer), I let the words of one of these psalms carry me into God's space. On good (and rare) days, I rest there. More often, I struggle there to quiet my heart enough to listen.

During the last four years of John's life, we often described our days as "bittersweet." Because of the fluctuations in the progress of his cancer, we lived a paradox of fear/hope, sorrow/joy, tears/laughter — sometimes simultaneously. We were adamant that we would not fudge the feelings, hide from the facts. Still, the facts and feelings kept shifting, forcing us to rely more and more on God and our love for one another. Neither failed us. Since no life is without recurring pain and pleasure, I hope that these psalms help you to take both to God. If you do, faith tells us that God responds.

God's response, of course, often deepens the paradox, but it seldom fails to comfort. When the loss of John seems to pull the air from my lungs, I sometimes feel a gentle presence that stays the panic. When narcissism narrows my sight, I find my eyes widening as I see again perspectives that shame my pettiness. So too, when grace or hormones raise my spirits, my joy doubles when I remember my God. The universality of these experiences guarantees that you know what I am saying. What John hoped you would also share is the conviction that God's response is not generic; rather, it is a unique expression of His infinite love for you.

God's love for us is the heart of the Christian mystery. What we call the "spiritual life" is but our effort to love God in return. John loved God fiercely. That love motivated his writing; drove his search for truth; sparked the play of our union. In the days before his death, we talked frequently about God. I sometimes vented my pain with remarks about "His" will being stupid as well as cruel or suggestions that God probably *is* male, since no woman would be so arbitrary. John would always smile, denying neither my anger nor my frustration. Soon though he would speak again about our common belief: that God is a mystery too good for us to comprehend. He would remind me that beneath feeling, beyond thought is the constancy of a God whose love is enfleshed.

Incarnation, Grace, and Trinity were the Christian mysteries that exercised John from his earliest studies of Karl Rahner and Bernard Lonergan. While he was composing these psalms, we were working on a manuscript we called *A Personal Christology*. Our reason for tackling this project was not primarily publication; rather, it was John's intuition that, since our days together were likely to be few, we should spend time reading the New Testament, drawing from it the strength we would need. I see in *God Is No Illusion* evidence of John's last probing of the synoptics and especially John, his favorite evangelist.

On August 31, 1995, about three weeks before he died, John wrote a meditation that he asked me to include in the program for his memorial Mass. He crafted it with the same care he gave his books. John wrote:

Increasingly, I have wanted to understand Christian life as a high comedy. The Incarnation being decisive, and the last things having been realized substantially, we can always try to work or suffer freely, and then join God in laughing. Worry does no good. Pain is crucifying but penultimate. The mournful tides of abandonment are just the way of common faith. We are most attractive when most eucharist — grateful for bread, wine, divine life. So, mischievously, I have been watching John the Baptist loose the thong of Jesus' sandal and the two of them amble down to the devil's grave. Magdalene strikes up a tune, and a little church starts to boogie barefoot.

I think this captures well both John's intention in the book and the faith that sustained his life and death.

A word about the dedication. John and I always devoted careful thought to our choices. As we neared the end of a manuscript, we would talk about to whom we might dedicate it and why: a friend's interest in the topic; her recent trouble that this book might assuage; his likely pleasure in seeing his name on the page. The dedications themselves carried no more than the names; we assumed that the recipients would understand. This time, however, I want to describe briefly the three men to whom this book is dedicated because, in different ways, each made its writing possible. Alfred Corn, a poet with the soul of a theologian, read the manuscript and encouraged John to publish it. Paul Crowley, S.J., a theologian with the soul of a poet, urged (hounded?) us to come to Santa Clara, where John spent his last year reveling in the beauty of the place and my delight with the university. Klaus Porzig, M.D., a Bay Area oncologist who accepted John as his patient and the two of us as friends, is the physician whose tender and wise care extended John's life. For each, John felt both gratitude and love. So do I.

DENISE LARDNER CARMODY
Santa Clara University
July 11, 1996

11

PREFACE

A prayerbook that I have used for many years offers a nice rendering of Job 14:7–12: "There is hope for a tree if it be cut down that it will sprout again and that its shoots will not cease. But a man dies and is laid low; a woman breathes her last and where is she? As a river wastes away and is dried up, so we lie down and rise not again" (Huub Oosterhuis, *Your Word Is Near* [New York: Newman, 1968], 76, adapted slightly).

Job is one of the Bible's spiritual heroes, refusing to accept the mere appearances of things. He wants a world in which there is justice. He keeps asking God to explain why what he experiences is so disordered. And beneath Job's demand that God defend the injustice of having stripped him of his health and wealth lies the invasive demand that many of us have felt at midnight, when it seems simply wrong, incompatible with "God," that poverty, sickness, infidelity, and unfairness of a dozen other kinds should slash so many people in our world. Indeed, the depth of any Jobian pursuit of theodicy takes us to our fundamental human mortality. We have to break down and die. That is the design that God has encoded in our genes, our bones, our blood. Why is this so? How can it be good — worthy of God? If you take either Job or the foundational issues in your own life seriously, these questions can haunt you.

The Christian response to Job, perhaps articulated most clearly in the Gospel of John and developed most systematically in the reflections of Eastern Orthodox theologians on *theosis* (divinization), is that the Word of God took flesh and died to give us human beings everlasting life. This radically good news can heal the profound depression that human suffering and dying threaten to visit to our souls. However, it takes most of us long years and numerous pains to become mature enough in our faith to make such a faith connatural, habitual, a stable disposition for our peace. Moreover, the Spirit of God tends to use the wisdom of a Job or a Qoheleth, the stoic biblical calls for minimalism and endurance, to keep us from any angelism about human mortality. The dark moods of Job should not be foreign to us. Nothing human should be foreign to us, if we follow a fully human God, a really crucified Lord, not letting ourselves blink away his scandal.

The prayers in this book are "psalms," songs of the deeper spirit sent out to God, in petition and adoration. Deliberately, I have tried to provide echoes of the canonical psalms of the Bible. I have more failed than succeeded, but just making the effort has been instructive. If there is a direction, a typical movement, in most of the biblical psalms, it is from lamentation to trust or praise. Certainly, some psalms are pure praise. But the majority begin with a cry of pain, a keening call for help. This starts a process of catharsis, because simply reaching out to God, displaying one's troubles, tends to remind one that God is powerful and good. Nothing earthly, not even one's pain or dying, is more ultimate than God. So making one's outcry to God quickly relativizes one's problems. God is mysterious, yes, but in the divine mystery there may well be salvation from our woes. What the synoptic gospels depict as miracles of Jesus and the Gospel of John depicts as signs are inducements to believe and hope that this could be so.

I have positioned these psalms so that the regular viewpoint is the end of life — serious illness, aging, death. The end of any venture casts light back upon the entire prior process, and anytime that we glimpse the end we get an invitation to judge how our pilgrimage is going. Kierkegaard has the rich observation that while life can only be lived forward, it can only be understood backward. The end that I have in view here, then, is the *telos* that Christians call God.

The subtitle makes these psalms an offering to the terminally ill. There is room for a *double entendre* or pun in this subtitle, since all human beings have death as their terminus, but my first connotation is more literal. If you begin to count the people you know whose hourglass is running out, you probably will run out of fingers and maybe also toes. Or you yourself may have a serious disease that makes your actuarial prospects dismal. Nowadays in just the United States tens of millions of people suffer from serious heart disease and terminal cancer. Lesser killers but still frightening foes run from AIDS to diabetes to multiple sclerosis to Parkinson's disease. Alzheimer's disease is in a class by itself, because it directly assaults human reason.

Many of the people brought close to the end, either physically or in imagination, whether through disease or other causes, find after the initial shock that they have been given an opportunity to deepen their appreciation of what human time can be for. If previously they had moved along unreflectively, living by the going values of their culture at large, they may well begin to think thoughts that are significantly counter-culture. American culture in the 1990s, for example, has become wonderfully broad and variegated, but pathetically narcissistic and shallow. So when death or pain or betrayal comes on the scene, dripping blood and breathing foul threats, the typical contemporary American worldling is like a sheep confronted with a slaughterer. No doubt that is the reason that the book chains sell so many brainless works on faith-cures, angels, miracles, carrot diets, and new age spirituality. People are desperate, so without even knowing it they sell their birthright for a mess of pottage.

The birthright bequeathed to all people formed in the Western cultures is a fine marriage of biblical and Hellenistic realism. In both of these foundational streams, such realism derives directly from contemplations of the human condition that stress its mortality, sinfulness, and passion for God. Thus the sober rumination that we have seen in Job. Thus the Platonic description of the love of wisdom as a practice of dying. And thus the late medieval focus of the *devotio moderna* on remembering death. Compared to this marrow of traditional Western culture (and one could bring forth solid analogues from India and China), the spate of recent books on easy cures for cancer, or finding orgasmic bliss without pain, or why smart women make dumb choices about men, or dieting your way to happiness are so superficial that they couldn't interest even a decent dermatologist. People aware of their mortality, and of the deep cracks in their culture, deserve infinitely better. Above all, those truly terminally ill, diagnosed as incurable, deserve something that does not insult their intelligence or gloss over the horrors they feel at 3:30 in the morning.

Last, the reader deserves to know that though I have a Ph.D. in religious studies that is not the competence on which I am drawing here. My postdoctoral preparation for this little book has been three and a half years living with multiple myeloma. Multiple myeloma is an incurable cancer of the bone marrow — a mindless cloning of excessive plasma cells that inevitably so destroys one's blood that one succumbs to infection or a cognate occasion. The mean time of survival after diagnosis is about three years. Diagnoses of multiple myeloma are on the rise these days, as are diagnoses of several other cancers. Presently in the United States there are about a thousand new cases reported each month. (For more information, call the International Myeloma Foundation at 1-800-452-CURE.) So my situation is hardly unique.

The psalms in this book come from thoughts of the late night and the early morning — times when I set out once again to sit alongside Job or found myself dumped there by pain. They are not heroic and they are not cheery — little nostrums cookie-cut by faith. I'm not even sure that they are honest, for they may owe as much to the writer in me as to the man with cancer and mottled faith. But they are what they are, and defects in their origin need not throw your use of them off-base. You can adapt them, correct them, reject them as you find good in your own dialogues with God. They are only stimuli, possibilities, grist for a personal religious mill. I hope that one or two of them may be of real use, for that would justify much of the pain behind them.

LETTER ONE

Good Friday/Easter Sunday 1992

Dear Friends,

Please excuse the generic character of this letter. We needed to contact quickly a limited circle of friends. Unfortunately, we have to impart some bad news.

I have bone cancer (multiple myeloma). The main locations seem to be the lower back and right leg, though the full extent is still being determined. I should begin chemotherapy next week. Presently this disease cannot be cured. However, the majority of patients respond favorably to chemotherapy, three years being the median survival.

You have been among the people who have graced our lives most intimately in the past. We hope that you will continue to do so in the future. Indeed, we'll rely on your reminding us that life is always short, so we should always live with intense gratitude for an inestimable gift, and that God is always long, so we should set no limits to our hopes. For now...

John and Denise

~ 1 ~

My God,
you are the Lord of life and death.
All seasons rest in your hand.
You number the hairs of our heads.
Not a sparrow flies,
not a leaf falls
apart from your providence.
Help me, then, my God,
for I feel abandoned.
My life makes little sense.
My mind spins, my spirit grows dizzy.
Around me babblers thrive.
They do not pray;
their works make no sense.
But you can draw my life from the pit.
Though the nations rage,
you move in full grace.
I am faithless and unstable.
You are always God.
What are we human beings
that you care for us?

~ 2 ~

Hasten, O God, to help me
for without you I am afraid.
Disease spreads in my bones.
Peace has vanished from my soul.
But you, O God,
can calm all storms.
Nothing in heaven or earth does not serve you.
When I consider your splendor,
the darkness from which the light comes,
I know that nothing will disturb me
if your hand holds me up.
If you love me,
no hatred of my enemies matters.
If you care for me,
death itself shrinks back.
There is no competition to you.
No law court or surgery ward
threatens your primacy.
Let all your people know this.
Then we may praise you suitably.
Then only you may provoke our songs.
All other gods are idols.

~ 3 ~

✦ Good God,
    is it wrong to hate my sufferings?
How ought I to think
about what strikes me down?
Your people have always had enemies.
From time out of mind
we have needed your help.
And you have responded.
Again and again
you have taken our turmoil away,
reduced our suffering and shame.
Do this now.
Be today our savior
as you have been in the past.
Are we less worthy,
less needy,
than the people you helped yesterday?
What are any of us
any day
that you care for our torment,
that you look upon us with pity?
You are the good God.
You love our kind.
Nothing that hurts us pleases you.
Show us the way forward.

LETTER TWO

May 11, 1992

Dear Friends,

Again, we apologize for using a generic letter, but it does save wear and tear. Thank you for your prayers and support — both are deeply appreciated.

On Wednesday, April 29, John was admitted to the hospital E.R. by ambulance, suffering from extreme lower back pain. X-rays showed two compressed vertebrae. On Thursday they operated, putting a two-foot rod in his right leg and a "nail" (spike) in his hip. These were to stabilize the leg which was about to break. On Thursday he also received the first (of ten) daily radiation treatments for the back, which they hope will alleviate some of the pain caused by the compressed vertebrae.

The effects of the previous week's intensive chemotherapy, the radiation sessions (he has the last three of the series this week), the operations on his hip and leg, *and* the physical therapy sessions in which he is learning to walk about made for a rough few days and nights. We both agreed that his birthday (May 3) was a memorable one!

Slowly, John is regaining his strength. The muscle spasms which had racked him are fewer, though still severe. We are both sleeping for longer stretches at night — Denise's being able to stay in John's room is a genuine blessing. While there are still problems (a persistent fever, a very low blood count — both of which have him in semi-isolation: no visitors or flowers), John's spirits and sense of humor remain high.

We rely on your prayers and appreciate your letters more than we can say. Please keep sending both. (Denise picks up the mail at the apartment each day and mail sent to the University of Tulsa reaches us regularly. Also, we can listen to any messages left on our home phone quite easily.)

We have one small problem. A few good friends, with the best intentions, have made their desire to know what is going on more imperative than our need to cope on a day by day basis. We're sure you'll understand, with a little reflection, that when the business of the day is getting through horrible hospital situations, we simply have no energy left over to meet those otherwise touching desires of our friends. We will tell you all that we can when we can. Please, please do not push us for more.

Gratefully,
John and Denise

~ **4** ~

✦ Day follows day to what purpose?
Where is all our toil to end?
Each night I fall to bed weary,
wondering what I have accomplished.
We all die,
and many of us are not happy.
Will you not redeem our lives from this pit?
Without your Spirit,
the love of your life in our hearts,
the most beautiful tree drops its branches,
the most graceful child turns gawky.
No one who thinks hard finds life easy.
Only a few sup on gilded plates.
You ask of us a great deal.
Just to keep going wears me out.
Once I thought my life would go simply
onward and upward and forward.
You have scrambled all my images,
turned my feet to backward alleys.
Still, though you slay me,
yet shall I trust you.
Though you break my bones,
I shall keep giving thanks.
For without you I am nothing.
With you I may possess all things.

~ 5 ~

Why do I feel abandoned?
Where has my sense that you support me gone?
Is my religion only good digestion?
When I feel bad am I bound to turn depressed?
I know that you are more than my feelings about you.
My mind says that you do not come and go.
But ill health can unhinge my mind,
make it seem no more trustworthy
than flights of imagination.
The just person lives by faith
below feelings, ideas, images
in a darkness that seldom fails.
The just person clings to your soleness.
O God, make me one of your just,
sure that there is no other God but you.
Though a thousand fall at my right side,
ten thousand be decimated at my left,
do you continue to be my creator,
my savior, redeemer, and Lord.
Grant all of us your Spirit.
In the cold of our deadly winters
have her warm our blood to survive.

~ 6 ~

You are light
in whom is no darkness at all.
You are love
free of all envy and hate.
You do not speak with a forked tongue.
You do not dissimulate
or offer false embraces.
All around me are liars and Pharisees,
godless people who do not ring true.
They hate my enjoyment of good times.
They love to see me fall down.
My God, my God,
why has it always been thus?
Who puts the envy in our drinking water?
How comes the resentment with our mothers' milk?
If now and then you did not send a mahatma,
we might think that all men had to be beasts,
all women were bound to be bitchy.
But one good person proves it is not so,
and so we have no excuse.
Save us, dear God, through this knowledge.
Assure us that even though our hearts condemn us,
even though our deaths mount the stairs,
you are greater.

~ 7 ~

Dear God,
how can I keep my hopes from flagging?
The medicines sap my energy.
The news trades in stupidity and violence.
If I look to either myself or humankind,
I see few reasons to keep going on.
But I can look outside, to you.
At any moment, I can drop my self-concern
and listen for your voice.
You are more than my lethargy.
Human stupidity does not defeat you.
The laughter of little children,
the thoughtfulness of good friends,
the constancy of my wife
remind me that your Spirit is powerful.
Show all your people your power.
Against our injustice and death
demonstrate again your might.
The inertia of our sins drags us down,
but our sins do not bind you.
Your ways are light and graceful.
Help us to choose your ways.
Send forth your angel.
Make it happen.
Give us good deaths.

LETTER THREE
June 1, 1992

Dear Friends,

This is the third of our generic letters we have designed to bring you abreast of the changes come upon us since mid-April, when a stranger knocked at our door, saying "Multiple myeloma is my name; overturning lives is my game."

Blessedly, our news this time is very positive. John is home from the hospital, virtually free of pain (thanks to radiation treatments), back to work, and continuing to progress beyond the level of fitness achieved through physical therapy in the hospital. Denise is thin but full of energy, overjoyed not to be sleeping at the hospital, amused, appalled, sobered, rendered not so much more or newly prayerful by the limp in John's walk, his snow-white hair, and the uncertain future that just these summer months portend, to say nothing of any longer vistas.

So we wait — for the next round of chemotherapy, for the fuller return of physical and mental strength, for the next indications of God's will — buoyed more than you will ever know by the flood of love, prayer, and simple thoughtfulness you have shown us. Unforgettably, we have learned we are not only saved by grace but also given full mail boxes, recording machines, and hearts wondering if previously they knew even the rudiments of what the word "friendship" denotes.

God bless you, and fill your cup to overflowing, for your goodness to us.

Love,
John and Denise

~ 8 ~

How happy and good it is
to gather together with friends,
to eat and drink and make merry
with people who strengthen our souls.
You have not made us solitary.
Apart from the vine we wither.
Gather us together this day
and make us your people again.
You know the storms raging against us.
Sickness and poverty and ignorance
afflict most of our kind.
If you do not take pity on us,
we are of all creatures under heaven
the most wretched and miserable.
But sometimes you do take pity.
As you choose
when you find it good
you place laughter and love in our midst.
So be for us, even in our last days,
a God of joy and life.

~ 9 ~

It is hard to grow old in this town.
Skin like lizards,
the rich come back from Acapulco
heavier drinkers than they went.
I watch and wonder
about their souls.
What do they expect from life,
from you?
What do I?
As one thing after another falls away
I sense how different you are.
The world turns
and we with it,
but you and suffering hold firm.
If I were wise,
I would set my soul on praising you
and so never run out of work.
The skin puckers,
the step and brain slow.
Only your silence stays young.

~ 10 ~

You let your people be treated badly.
Friend after friend has a sad tale to tell.
The wrong people are in charge,
venal and unimaginative.
Has it always been this way?
I do not understand why.
What is so hard about telling the truth,
keeping one's word,
remembering how pain feels?
Why do you not smite the wicked,
teach the obtuse by slashing their flesh?
In your silence, God, you seem not to care
and so to sanction the status quo.
I hate the ways of the wicked,
and I want you to hate them too.
Rise up, O God,
and show yourself our savior.
If you do not judge
between sinners and the righteous,
how will we bear the moral life?
O God of our dying,
be our just judge.

~ 11 ~

✦ Praise in high heaven
and praise here on earth far below.
You, our God,
deserve all honor and glory and power and might
for there is none like you.
Of all the gods only you
do not disappoint us.
Only you abide in all places, all times
come rain, come shine, come woe.
Be gentle toward our weakness.
You know we cannot understand
and do not do well with pain.
If we were running creation
we think a great deal would be easier.
We would not go to bed afraid.
But without you we are nothing,
less than tiny specks in chaos's swarm.
It is well that we are not running creation.
It is best that we need entrust all things to you.
Into your hands, then,
we commend our spirits.
Into your providence
we abandon ourselves.

~ 12 ~

Where are my last days taking me,
I ask you, God of my time?
When I seek your face
what does my soul pursue?
You have placed me here,
given me x length of days
but what do you want me to accomplish?
Why have you breathed into my dust a spirit?
Once I knew the answers to these questions.
Years ago everything seemed clear.
Now I know nothing for certain.
All around me and in me is dark.
I think that this has been progress.
I'm glad that I've unlearned so much.
Now I'm readier for the problems of midnight,
the ones requiring strength of soul.
We do much less than is done to us.
We undergo much more than we accomplish.
Today I ask only to say, "Thank you."
Tomorrow can take care of itself.

~ 13 ~

✦ I have enemies,
  and the plain fact shocks me.
I have not moved against any of your people,
yet some hate me in their hearts.
They want no one to stand against their chiseling.
Their deeds are evil
so they flee the light.
"Fool," they say in their heart,
"there is no God."
My mind reels, my tongue turns to ashes
when I consider the enormity of their sin.
You have made them for yourself.
Their hearts are restless till they rest in you.
But they reject what you have made them.
They lie and cheat and philander
because they are shamefully weak.
Rise up, O God, against them.
Do not let their ways prevail.
If you do not assert what is right,
do not stand behind your light
who will defend your name?
Teach me, my God, your ways.
Show me how to deal with your enemies.
Should I denounce them
or pray that you forgive them
because they know not what they do?

~ 14 ~

Another day ends imperfect.
Another examination of conscience
shows much to confess.
You have made us much less than angels.
Error is our middle name.
Can we assume, then, that you are patient?
Do our faults matter less than our love?
Now that I am sick unto death
I feel little temptation to perfectionism.
Often I just want to give up.
I am weary morally as well as physically.
It is a great effort even to care.
If you want your will done in me,
you will have to do it yourself.
If you require satisfactory prayer,
it will have to come from your Spirit.
My spirit is as weak as my flesh.
I do well to thank you for small blessings.
Yet the smoking flax you do not quench.
The bruised reed you do not break.
And the tired, discouraged sinner?
Look not, O God, at our failures
but at the faith of your saints.
See what the few successful among us
have accomplished
and let that cover the rest.

~ 15 ~

✦ Around me,
  complainers pollute the air.
The more advantages they receive
the less work they want to do.
It is an unattractive human trait —
thinking oneself put upon —
for it shows a deep forgetfulness
of what being a creature means.
We have no rights against you.
We have not advanced one step beyond Job.
If you do not hold us in being,
we fall back into nothingness.
If you take note of our sins,
we end up in outer darkness
weeping and gnashing our teeth.
O God,
give me a simple spirit
of contentment and gratitude.
Help me to see utterly clearly
that all my life has been grace.
If you ask me to suffer,
so be it.
Only give me the grace
to carry it through well.

~ 16 ~

In deepest night the morning star
begins the shift of forces.
We are never closer to you
than when we feel farthest apart.
You want us, God,
for yourself,
though you envy none of our possessions.
You want us to be as you have made us
desire without limit or lust.
In your divinity, God,
you break down all barriers.
The closer we come to you
the more fully we become ourselves.
You are not our competition,
much less our enemy.
You are completely free
letting your sun shine,
your rain fall
on just and unjust alike.

LETTER FOUR

September 21, 1992

Dear Friends,

Lately we've gotten a spate of inquiries about how things are going, so — herewith generic letter #4.

Denise is back to school and very busy, but in good spirits, both because I am doing well and because her new dean shows promise of leading the faculty out of some of the swamps in which they've slogged the last few years.

My blood, monitored twice a month, shows a good return to health: white counts okay, hemoglobin 13.3, etc. The aberrant protein marker has fallen from an initial 5.0 to 2.3 to 1.7 and now is 1.8 — signs the chemotherapy has done some good. I swim a mile every other day. For two months I've been walking (lurching) without a cane. I can work almost to normal measures. My disposition is sweet as ever. I have gained back the twenty pounds I lost in the hospital (see Leviticus 3:16: "All fat is the Lord's"). My lower back and right leg remain sore, but not impossibly so. For the present I'm doing one (seven-day) session of chemotherapy a month. All that is said about prednisone is true — an impressive drug, not always pleasant. But the chemotherapy has not become a bugbear (e.g., no violent nausea).

Mental matters are interesting, now that crisis has taken a break and a quasi-normal health returned. The cliché about living one day at a time doesn't cover the whole, but it can cover a lot. Most days I'm content to let all of the future as well as all of the fat belong to God. Now and then I'm aware that terrible things happen to God's people, near and far, and that God bears a heavy responsibility, something not to be fobbed off on secondary causes. On the other hand, remembering Job, I find myself waiting and hoping for the revelation of how all God's ways are ways of love, which has to be, if "God" is going to be anything worth believing in, longing for.

Many times Denise and I have felt your prayers and good wishes nearly palpably. The communion of saints, all of us sinners, is no illusion. So the main function of this little letter is to thank you for all your help, and to ask you humbly to stay with us.

Much love,
John and Denise

~ 17 ~

How good and happy it is,
for friends to laugh at their troubles,
share warmth at the pot-bellied stove.
We believe in you together,
and this makes our time funny.
You hold us and save us and raise us up
so nothing bad is final.
You are the first and the last.
We are only the intermediate.
You matter wholly and completely.
We matter very little.
It is delicious to matter little —
a cold, clear drink of water.
It is exhilarating to have you increase,
feel our egos grow small and quiet.
O God, God, God —
the one we have to hold on to.
Burn yourself into our souls.
Come at our waking
and do not go when we sleep.
What else is there for us?
Who else never falters?
In the beauty of the lilies
and the horror of depression
and the gentle lapping of the last waves
you are enough.

~ 18 ~

When the body revolts
and the head aches
and the stomach wretches,
I think of how you have made us
open to microbes, viruses, mistakes.
We are flesh easily wounded
matter prone quickly to bleed.
You have to know this,
take it into account,
use it to feel tender toward us.
We are not much
to look at or appreciate or love.
We can be the apple of your eye
only if you think of us as flesh of your flesh,
fruit of your love.
Do think of us this way
and open up the world for us.
Let us roam like privileged scions,
princesses free and unspoiled.
Let us live
along your lakes and streams
as though we had named all the animals —
the lion to lie down with the lamb,
the asp to play second base.

~ 19 ~

Peace to your people on earth.
Let all with hate in their hearts
lay down their arms,
return to their shops and fields.
Let parents take back their children,
women forgive their men.
No longer should color or language,
age or class,
douse your people in bile.
Stop our angry mouths, O God,
quiet our envious spirits.
When you make yourself our treasure,
the sun glinting off the waters,
we have little reason to fight.
When your Spirit carries our spirit
with signs too deep for words,
we feel most of our conflicts are futile.
By raging we cannot add
a single cubit to our status.
By possessing our souls in patience
we can see the roof come off high
heaven,
hear the seraphim sing.
Alone in the alcoves of cathedrals
sages dance on their knees.

~ 20 ~

✦ The prick of misfortune
like the prick of the intravenous needle
can alter our substance,
work for our good.
That we may believe this
show us your providence —
how pain has helped us grow.
Until I was bone weary
my heart seldom went out
to street people, mothers, or clerks.
Until my brain reeled from chemicals
I could not imagine
what it is like to be stupid,
unfocused and confused.
Am I better because now my shoulders slump,
my brain can go addled and banal?
Maybe, my God, I've become more like you,
more tolerant, patient, understanding.
As you break down my health
make me like you more.

~ 21 ~

✠ You number our days,
 and the proteins in our marrow.
Nothing happens to us globally
or in any particular part
that you do not direct and decide.
Fools say in their hearts
no God works in the universe.
Believers find you working everywhere,
nothing not impressed with your thumb.
I want to believe this;
help thou my unbelief.
I want to trust that no matter what happens
you rule our lives on earth.
We cannot avoid pain or dying.
The question is simply when.
We have to give our selves over
and the better we do it the wiser.
If we need a fish,
we should not fear a scorpion.
If we know how to give our children good things,
you have to treat us well.

~ 22 ~

✦ Give us, O God, some truly religious leaders,
   sages to guide us in your ways.
It should not be so difficult
to find shepherds of faith, integrity, brains.
What do the ones we have do all day?
How do they spend their resources?
A middling talent could clean up most messes
quickly, calmly, sweetly.
When will you take pity
and send some talent our way?
Then we might walk around more disasters,
head off more pains before they happened.
Sun Tzu and Machiavelli knew this.
Is it too much to ask in the church?

LETTER FIVE

January 15, 1993

Dear Friends,

The news over the past few months has been good, help-ing us to end 1992 with peace, if not gratitude, and to begin 1993 hopefully. We extended our circle of venturesomeness bit by bit through travel: Austin in October, San Francisco in November, Europe (Austria and France) in early January. Each trip proceeded without untoward incident, helping us to feel that we were edging back toward normalcy. The biweekly lab reports say that my blood is doing well, both white fel-lows and red fellows, and that the serum protein marker for the myeloma has been descending (1.5, 1.4, 1.2), as it does when chemotherapy is effective. (Chemotherapy will probably continue for another year.) A visit to the surgeon just before Christmas revealed that the bone in my right leg, on which he operated at the end of April, has continued to grow back well and is now nearly fully restored. Therefore I do not have to see him again for a year, barring bad new eventualities. A brace greatly helps my broken back, while the rod in my leg gives no sharp pain, only light habitual stiffness and soreness. We have much progress, then, for which to be grateful.

The mental or spiritual challenge, for both us and people beholding us from the outside, seems to have shifted so that now it is to hold to a sharp line at the border of crisis and nor-malcy. (The last chapters of Arthur Frank's *At the Will of the Body* treat this well.) On the one hand, nothing has changed in the core diagnosis: I have an incurable cancer of the bone marrow, the statistics on which give a mean life expectancy of less than three years from the time of discovery (mid-April 1992). Thus we would be foolish not to see these current months as time shadowed by the advent of God. On the other hand, I have responded very well to the chemotherapy, and the days apart from its baleful effects can be splendid: decent work, significant physical exercise, lots of laughs, moments of quiet awareness of beautiful ultimacy. Denise and I will collaborate in teaching an evening course this semester, beginning Monday. Our books continue to assemble themselves on schedule: five or six should come out in '93, one or two of them on dying and death. So the shadow is not debilitating, as it is not disheartening.

Thanks, once again, for all your interest, love, and support, which have greatly helped us to keep heart. Please continue to hold us in your prayers, as we hold you in ours.

Love,
John and Denise

~ 23 ~

At night I hear people crying,
a lament rising up from pain.
They are your people;
please hear their cries and help them.
Some hurt down to their bones.
Others are lonely or feel worthless.
A few have good friends for support,
but a great many have only you.
Where are you?
Why are you so hard to find?
We want you to be our God,
but you seem uncertain you want to.
We want you to wipe away our tears,
but I still hear Rachel weeping
and sometimes I join her in chorus.
Teach us again how to laugh.
Show us once more life's comedy.
Let us eat, drink, and make merry
to your praise and glory.
It does you no honor to slay us.
From the doldrums we sing only sad songs.
Let us sing songs of plenty.
Give us good reasons for cheer.

~ 24 ~

I don't know which is wearier,
my body or my spirit.
The disease eats at my bones,
the medicines wipe me out.
But missing you
is the heavier burden.
When I feel that my pains are your will,
something you want to redeem,
they are not hard to carry.
When I find in them no sense,
they seem only destructive.
I want to cry out in frustration
for all the wrong in the world.
We are small people, God,
as easily rolled up and crushed as paper.
The longest of our lives
does not last one of your seconds.
Hold us close then in your meaning
lest we feel terribly badly made.
Help us to believe
deep in our souls
that you have purposes for our dying
and you let nothing decent be lost.

~ 25 ~

✦ Great numbers of people suffer physical pain;
worry bends myriads more.
You have made a world
that only a few find easy.
Before they reach the grave
the majority have cried many nights.
I have given up asking why you have done this.
Your reasons remain as obscure as your self.
You are too much for me to fathom.
I have no insight into your plan.
But I love the beauty of your dawning,
the light coming into my conscience at prayer.
And I am grateful for your peace at midnight
inviting me to resignation.
Deep in the wastes of space
everything witnesses to your necessity.
You have done what you have done
for reasons all your own.
I want to say amen to it
though the coldness frightens me terribly.
I want to embrace your will,
come sun or rain or storm.

LETTER SIX
April 15, 1993

Dear Friends,

The past three months have moved quickly, and well. My medical condition has been stable — good blood work, fair (now normal) energy. We have been busy with visitors (three stimulating lecturers, two Warren and one Snuggs), trips (weekends in Dallas and Wichita/Lawrence), work at the university (the evening class that we've taught together has gone well and been a lot of fun), and books (the third edition of our text on Christianity; proofing: the *Festschrift* for Bob Brown, the book on Buddha-Confucius-Jesus-Muhammad, and the book on Native American religions — a muchness to make the eyes bleary). Looking ahead, we see the Catholic Theological Society's meeting in San Antonio in mid-June, a trip to the West Coast in later June (the center of which will be a week's teaching at USF), and three weeks from the end of July to mid-August on the East Coast to see family and kiss the sand at Gloucester. Those are nice scenes to foresee.

Some of you are well aware that yesterday marked the anniversary of the diagnosis of my multiple myeloma. It has been a strange year, with many of the details now vague (to me; nothing is vague to Denise), apparently lost to a largely beneficent fog. I hope it is that cloud of forgetting that the mystics encourage, as well as a natural psychosomatic response to pain. We do not forget, however, the kindness many of you have shown us, nor the palpable lift of your prayers. There is a communion of saints, and it includes many who might not be comfortable being named members. Sorry, what you do and are has the say in that, not the uniform in which you feel comfortable. We also remember the times during the past year when we have felt freest, gathering them now into a vivid memory that becomes a resolution: with time probably short, we should live well, as though Irenaeus were right and the glory of God were human beings fully alive.

So we ask you: Help us to become more fully alive, more sensitive and grateful, as we promise to help you. You know, at least as well as we, that the life, the vitality, most worth wanting comes from love — the love that Dante saw moving the stars, the love that the Song of Songs knows is strong as death. Love helps us endure suffering, from time to time even gracefully, and it is from love that resurrection breaks forth. Indeed, love is an arrabon, a down-payment on heaven (a taste of divine Spirit). This Easter, for a little while, a spirit of peace and joy wiped every tear from our eyes, and death was no more. We felt that you, all that we love, were close, and that none of us was alone. Bless you, in the beauty of the lilies.

Love,
John and Denise

~ 26 ~

✦ The seasons sing your praises,
　　the flowers and animals and fields,
the skies and rocks and waters,
the people who have any sense.
You are our source,
the mind that makes us move,
the power that gives us being,
the goodness for which we hope.
We cannot go anywhere that you are not present,
no time or space or mood.
You are the best of our mothers,
the first of our fathers,
the lover most exciting our hearts.
In the morning you give us courage and hope;
at night you hush us to peace.
I love you as the beauty that might be,
the passion pure and fertile,
the healing of the wounded,
the protection of all the hurt.
You feed my mind and draw my eye;
your harp soothes my inner ear.
You are everything that I want,
all that I need,
so I beg you:
let me go to you well.

~ 27 ~

The worse our health or turmoil
the more our prayers to you change.
Troubled people have little stability.
We move up, down, to the side
all in the same day.
Can you smile that we are so flighty
and not be put off by our skittishness?
Can you wait patiently
for maturity to overtake us?
O God, you have been waiting
since first we came out of the womb.
We have lived hither, yon, two towns over
the entirety of our conscious life.
So be in the depths of our spirits
where you hold back the void,
our rock, fortress, salvation,
a vane stable in all weathers.
Be yourself our constancy.
Keep us yourself from hopeless idolatry,
the inflation and deflation that toss us up and down.
And at our end
take us to yourself
with whom there is no variation or instability.

~ 28 ~

If my soul were well ordered,
I would not care
how my fortunes evolved.
I would want only to praise your name.
But how can I know
what praises your name,
what the nations are actually singing?
I believe that the tides move without fail
and that your programs direct the embryos.
But the peoples, Lord, the peoples
and I in my pride
and the fools who shout on Wall Street—
how can you depend on us?
If our souls were well ordered,
we would rise early,
psalms on our lips,
praise in our hearts like honey.
We would succor the lame, the halt, the blind.
We would study nature and human beings slowly,
relishing insight, possibility, faith.
We would seek your face
this day and always
world without end. Amen.

~ 29 ~

I wonder about worry,
how it works in your plan,
what is the best way to use it
and the best way to throw it away.
Imperfect in faith
I do sometimes worry,
wonder in panic
whether you have withdrawn your hand.
Yet all things return to you
sooner or later
more or less gracefully.
And so I know now my terminus,
where I shall finish,
the end of my little train's line.
Only the hour and mode are obscure.
Help us, we pray,
to trust in your guidance,
cling to your promises,
hold to your love.
Grant to our friends,
all those who love us,
about whom we worry,
full freedom in faith.
They cannot safeguard our lives
as we cannot safeguard theirs.
Strong, then, are the grounds for our worry
and stronger the grounds for tossing all worry away.

~ 30 ~

✦ Let there be praise on Sion
   in all houses of worship,
all homes where children kneel before going to bed,
all porches where lovers swing to the stars.
Worthy are you, God, of all praise
honor, glory, power, might,
for you are the first and the last,
the one and the only,
the best and surest
we ever have had.
May we praise you in good times
and in bad times praise you more.
May we praise you for your gifts
and for your plain self even more.
Make it our cornerstone
that you simply are.
Make it our steeple
that you are good.
Grant to your mature in faith,
those who live in the eye of the storm,
the grace no longer to reason at length.
Let them take their lives like bread
from your motherly hand.

~ 31 ~

I am learning
   that I must let myself go,
drift out on your darkness,
sail along by the stars.
Nothing and no one
can assure me about you.
You have to be
your own guarantor.
So I pray:
Do not baby me
but remember my weakness,
giving me the diet
my soul needs each now.
Sharpen my mind,
anneal my soul,
stimulate my endorphins
to hold off my pain.
I know that I am dying
and I want to go well
but not without carrying
her whom I love.
So grant in your heaven
loving and marrying
an endless unfolding
of what began well
in flesh you took to yourself
to dwell among us
and die to defeat our death.

~ 32 ~

✦ Absorbed with the possibility of you
I wait, sometimes in joyful hope
for the coming of my savior
however you make that to be.
I wait
realizing that I have always been waiting
my ear cocked at midnight,
my soul arrested in a permanent pause.
In my beginning was your word
or your silence before it
or the grand quiet into which all things recede.
In the beginning only you are
holding all initiative
and without you there is nothing,
no world and no me.
I come from you as directly as the world does.
You say let there be or I am not even a glimmer
and for as long as I am
you keep saying my name.
Let me rest in your saying,
flow out on your speaking
define my existence as a particle of your word.
Let me think of myself
as an effect of your thinking,
engaging your mind for as long as I am.
If in my name there is any light,
in my self any meaning
it comes only from your remembering
to hold me in being,
only from your willingness
to keep saying my name.

~ 33 ~

Beyond feeling,
there where neither pain nor joy has an address,
I lay thick, insensitive hands
on your delicate being,
the lover's self you reveal then and now.
How ought we dying to manage
when nothing is fine,
all delicacy mocks us,
we slide and slip and slide on gray vomit?
What ought we to say
to the pretty little writers, who go on so preciously
about care of the soul?
You are not pretty, God,
and many of your people are writhing.
Sometimes I want to smash those little writers,
make sure they at least know rudimentary pain.
So free yourself from all of us,
us who abuse you.
In your terrible transcendence
stand far, far apart.
Be as different from us as you can be
without breaking us into little pieces.

LETTER SEVEN
July 15, 1993

Dear Friends,

We have finished the school year well, enjoyed trips to Des Moines, San Antonio, and the West Coast (where the excuse was a week's teaching at the University of San Francisco), gotten some good writing done, and learned that a new phase of therapy is about to begin.

The standard chemotherapy for my multiple myeloma has worked well but probably reached the point of diminishing return (where possible damage to the bone marrow offsets damage to the cancer). My oncologist's advice therefore is to stop the chemotherapy and see what the myeloma does, perhaps in the meanwhile taking interferon (which seems to prolong the remission of some people with my profile). Psychologically, the prospect of quitting the drugs is attractive, but with their going we lose a safety net. Now there is only my natural defenses (probably plus the interferon), your prayers, and the providential designs of God.

Of course, all of us live by the providential designs of God, whether we think we read them in hematological graphs or not. "Number our days," we ask now and then, when we sense that time unnumbered would be meaningless. For a few of you, I have survived for sufficient time to no longer be a news item, a tragedy or curiosity worth your bothering about. For far more of you, the will to offer overt support, renewed promises of prayer, has continued strong, much to our benefit and gratitude.

Day by day, the little colony of us — changed, shaped,

colored by an aberrant mechanism in my marrow — go our way, barely discernible among the world's billions, in whose midst the providence of God rules things more dramatically. When I pray for you, I'm very conscious of this daily disposition of being, life, grace — "bread," the prayer of Jesus calls it. When I feel so bold as to specify what God ought to do for you, I usually ask for abandonment. May you feel, down to your marrow, that nothing is casual, haphazard, meaningless — not because the world makes great sense, but because the mystery of God is always great, the death and resurrection of Christ are always a symbolism more primordial. May you trust this mystery, this symbolism, and surrender yourself to what will be.

Blessings on your summer. More later about my book *How to Handle Trouble,* which I hope will redeem some of the bad times Denise and I have been through, through the good offices of Doubleday, who to this point have avoided bathos and kept good taste. Our thanks, again, and our love.

John and Denise

~ 34 ~

 Perhaps some people can live well without you,
their neglect of "God" honest and unquestioned.
I cannot,
have not been able
since first I came to reason
nearly fifty years ago.
For decades I have wanted you
with a child's lisping passion
crying in my bed
for you to wipe my tears away.
I knew far too early
from precocious wounding
that all life is suffering
and the cause is desire.
But I've never been sure that
desire isn't the remedy also,
desire made pure by a dazzling beauty,
a love that would ask all
and on occasion provide all
that we or it ever could ask.
Can I find this love now
in the rotting of my flesh,
the throb of my bones,
the much greater throb of my angel's heart?
Please, please let it be so.

~ 35 ~

We hear horrible stories about the children,
what is happening to them through famine and war.
Millions go without adequate food and clothing,
millions more get no good health care or education.
How can people do this to their own flesh and blood?
How can you let this happen
to the most obvious citizens of heaven?
So let us pray for those who care for the children:
mothers and fathers,
grandmothers and grandfathers,
sisters and brothers,
aunts and uncles,
teachers and doctors and coaches and nurses,
all who have taken the next generation to heart.
You, God, have given us life;
we ask you now to safeguard it.
In the miracle of each birth
you make us a pledge;
we ask you now to keep it.
And, of course, we make pledges too.
So we ask you now to help us keep them.
Teach us a responsible birth control.
Help us to love and cherish
all whom we bring into life.

~ 36 ~

At your judgment
we shall receive our deserts.
Help us to wait for that day
not worrying prematurely,
doing what we can,
letting other things go.
Seldom do human affairs unfold fully justly.
Lies ripple near, far, and wide.
Many good deeds go unnoticed
unrewarded, unappreciated.
We do well to keep living forward toward you,
not caring what our neighbors say.
We do well to treasure
high in our bank vault
a conscience peaceful in your sight.
You alone will not fail us.
Always your mystery will continue to stand
before us, behind us, below and above.
Help us to live in your mystery.
Make yourself our one true home.

~ 37 ~

Come in the splendor of your storm,
O God of lightning and might.
Your power crackles through the sky
yet also moves delicately
in every leaf, drop, and cell.
You move equally delicately
in the rivulets of our souls.
In corners of our passion,
tiny patches we have not covered up,
you hush and cajole and seduce us
to be what we ought and want.
But your ways
are not our ways
as the heavens are not the earth.
You answer to no one outside you,
Lord and everyone's master.
Strange, then, that you make yourself vulnerable,
hang on our words, wait for our yes.
How do you do this?
By what mechanism do you assure
that we always stay free?
We come to ourselves so seldom
that usually we are run by desire.
We want and fear so strongly
that seldom do we know
the things for our peace.
But you, God, can defeat our compulsions.
You can take us to yourself
and set our souls free.

~ 38 ~

What is your glory?
How should we imagine it
and draw from it strength?
Is it the light of a thousand suns,
the purest chords of the purest harpists,
the feel of sable, linen, or silk?
Is it the "objective correlative" of our holiest awe,
what we want and honor when we love you completely,
the fire for our souls' best sandalwood?
Your glory is not this and not that.
It is nothing we can picture or touch or comprehend.
Your glory like yourself is beyond words,
primal primitive its own signifying.
We honor it best by simply chanting your name:
Holy Holy Holy,
a mantra most soothing,
a harmonic fit for the simplest soul.
"God" is as good as "Glory" or "Holy."
Neither of the three ever makes the other ones plain.
Nothing ever makes you plain, clear, obvious.
Always you only are.
Be patient, then, when this defeats us.
Be patient with us this day and always
world without end. Amen.

~ 39 ~

✦ I see the face imprinted in the towel
of El Greco's Veronica.
I think of the thorns
and the trickles of blood
and migraines of the soul.
Here is an image
for all of our suffering
all the lamentation,
of all of our psalms.
Here is our flesh
split down to purple
showing inside
the whites of the bones.
Behold the man.
Behold my self,
the neighbor round the corner,
the idiot one over in the next stinking cell.
Do you see us, God?
Do you let the reek of us reach you?
Oh, oh, oh,
we rock back and forth moaning.
O God, incline unto our aid.
O Lord, make haste to help us.
Who but you can save us?
Where else do we have to go?

~ 40 ~

I watch your people at the hospital,
huddled in our waiting area
wondering what their next procedure will require,
afraid of the pain, the expense, the bad news.
We all have bones that break,
blood that goes out of balance,
organs that quit or turn us against ourselves.
We all age
or lose our defenses
or feel our will to live slipping away.
We are each both a wonder,
a series of high improbabilities,
and a tragedy always about just to happen.
Our bodies,
like the pond visible through the window
and the flowers winding down the hill,
tell us that life is precious
and ought constantly to dazzle our souls.
On good days we agree,
singing benison after benison,
to the goodness of your name.
On bad days we wonder
and draw our hope back into our dank little shells.
When the pain mounts up our neck
and begins to drill into our brain,
we ask why you have made us this way.
But you do not answer.
You make us wait to cross a trickling Jordan.

~ 41 ~

We live in the midst of sinners
and the midst of a sinful self.
We choose to be stupid and slow,
self-centered and closed
to your beauty.
The world around us in nature,
the world that our infants scan,
calls us to light and understanding,
promising that you are its reason and form.
Where does that world go?
How do we lose
our passion for reason and form?
Torpor settles upon us
and we draw it over our shoulders
like a soft favorite blanket.
We don't want to bestir ourselves,
deny ourselves,
keep moving out to a better center.
So you have to afflict us
with pain and disappointment.
Prosperity is usually bad for our souls.
O God, have you made us so poorly
that to find ourselves we have to misfire?
Is our being so paradoxical
that we have to sin to feel your grace,
die to gain everlasting life?

~ 42 ~

The women wallow in dependence,
and the men lust for control.
More of us miss you
than hit your mark,
the golden mean of your freedom.
The closer we come to you
the more we become ourselves.
The greater our desire to hand ourselves over
the richer our self-possession.
You hold the selves that we glimpse
when the moon hangs low for harvest.
You move us not to care —
to let anxiety, greed, self-importance go.
But be you then all important to us
so we may suffer less from our very sick selves.
Help us not to care overmuch
about the good opinion of our brothers,
the pleasurable compliance of our sisters,
the surety of our own place in the sun.
Take us by the hand,
neurotic though we be,
and wash every stain from our souls.

LETTER EIGHT
October 15, 1993

Dear Friends,

We have a mixed report. The cancer has come back, with some vigor, so I have resumed chemotherapy. At the end of the first course of chemotherapy, in May of 1993, the protein marker had shrunk to 1.0, from the original 5.0 of April 1992. From May to October 1993, when first I took nothing and then, for the last six weeks, took interferon, the marker rose steadily: 1.2, 1.7, 2.0, 2.7. So last week I began a new chemotherapy (pills) stressing high steroids: dexamethasone (brand-name decadron), combined with melphalan (alkeran). Each twenty-eight-day period I do three sets of four days of drugs and four days off. The first four days each "month" stipulate 14 mg melphalan and 40 mg dexamethasone. The second and third four days are only the 40 mg of dexamethasone. After day 20, I take seven or eight days off. Dr. Raymond Alexanian, a leading expert on myeloma, based at M. D. Anderson in Houston, has recommended this regime for me. The most dangerous side-effects possible are osteoporosis, cataracts, and necrosis of the femoral head. The four-day breaks, along with the limited duration planned (six months), should offset these dangers.

At this point I have completed only one eight-day fraction of a cycle. It has gone well — nothing horrible. I find myself grateful that we are attacking the cancer, rather than just waiting. True, the cancer and I are becoming familiars, slipping all too easily into waltz time; right now, though, we're calling the tunes. Also, I have been getting useful thoughts

75

about the presence of God in destruction. What breaks down our resistances to God's love? How does death function to bring us to our beloved, whom prior to death we can usually only wait upon in faith? Elizabeth of the Trinity reminds me that a radical faith goes well below feelings. I don't know whether I shall be able to hold to this reminder in sharp pain, but at the moment it is useful. It doesn't matter what I think or feel about God. God is God regardless. But I can pray to God to let me want God's triumphing, condensing this prayer into a simple "amen." And so can you, for both yourself and us. The fact is that there is almost only God — our human reality is paper thin. In physical destruction we get to feel this thinness and the inevitability of our breakup, which can bring a new hopefulness about death. The flesh of Christ was bound for physical destruction. It could never avoid that destiny. However, believers think that the dying of Christ destroyed death — the agency of destruction had the tables turned, the cancer was consumed. You see the bent of a classical theological education.

Doubleday says that *How to Handle Trouble* will be a selection of the Book-of-the-Month Club, and in the spring Twenty-Third Publications will bring out *Cancer and Faith*. Ironic but consoling.

Love,
John and Denise

In my bones things are breaking.
The marrow does not hold.
You have made us mortal, God,
and inexorably this comes home.
Is there anything in us not passing,
anything stable that endures?
In the depths of our spirit
when nothing is left but love,
do you hold us in your deathlessness?
Grant us, O God, to feel that you do
so we have reasons to keep on trying.
Let us imagine that we are of a sort
that we go to a place
that will keep us real for our children.
This passing place here below,
this space and time and dying,
is good enough in its own way.
We should be grateful to have been born,
to have laughed and worked and wept.
But we are more than our pain,
more than our joy,
more than all that is passing.
The spark you have placed in our clod
is a diamond harder than death.
Do not deny the way you have made us.
Join us to Jesus,
the first-born from the dead.

~ **44** ~

It is evening,
  the light slanting low.
I am tired
like most of your people.
Even the life of a sick little drone
siphons energy away.
On the bad days
just holding myself together,
sustaining a minimum of hope,
is exhausting,
and they are becoming more frequent.
You ravish us, O God,
steadily, surely, without any remorse.
But our end is in our beginning
if we can outwit the melancholy.
So help us to do what we can
which is less than we might have
but more than our critics expect.
We can leave a greasy mark
on one or two pillows,
put a nick in one or two hearts,
but it is you who justify us.
In the wilderness of your justice
we huddle together terribly small.
You have to know this, O God.
Please act upon it
and take us to your heart.

~ 45 ~

In their fat stupid laziness
the heathen ruin your world.
Everything coming from them is slanted,
cut on a bias of self-service.
I have no words for dealing with them.
They speak a foreign language.
In their mouths nothing means what it ought,
nothing carries commitment,
everything wastes my time.
How do unbelievers think about time?
Is it simply for getting through?
Time ought to be our dearest treasure,
chance after chance to listen for your Word.
If today you speak your Word,
if now becomes an acceptable hour,
harden not our hearts or our minds.
Rather, give us your Spirit of acceptance.
The heathen will always despise us,
understand us no better than we understand them.
The ugliness of their ways will always curl our lip
and this they will never forgive us.
So are we bound to live at daggers drawn
like Jesus and the Pharisees.
In your mercy, God,
keep us from useless pride
but also from silly illusion:
The heathen are mortal enemies.

LETTER NINE

January 31, 1994

Dear Friends,

The new chemotherapy that we described in the last letter has worked well, in three courses reducing the protein spike from 2.7 to 1.5. I'll probably do a few more cycles. The side effects have not been bad.

We've traveled an unusual amount in the past three months: Wichita and Lawrence, Washington, D.C. (AAR), Jerusalem (Jewish-Christian-Muslim trialogue), Palo Alto (party for R. M. Brown *Festschrift*), and (John) Washington, D.C. (International Myeloma Foundation — Patients' Seminar). Each trip has brought different benefits and several were full of grace.

As my bone marrow gets pounded down, I sometimes feel like Paul's pot, being worked out by the divine potter. I think of clay, ashes, dust — variants of the nothingness of the creature, experienced as liberating. It feels good not to have to matter, except to the mercy of God. It feels fortunate in my bones to escape from the narcissism so thick on the ground, in my past biography.

There have been billions of us thinking, sorrowing human creatures, since our kind began hundreds of thousands of years ago, a genetic sport. What do any of us matter, unless God beholds us as the apple of his eye and wants to wipe away our every trouble? Yes, trouble is legion, as most of you know, unfortunately. But trouble shared, as Denise and I know so fortunately, is trouble halved and humanized. So speak your troubles out, and let them go.

We who try to be Christians are wisest and happiest, I find, when, in virtue of Jesus, we do let our troubles go, all our self-concern, and allow our passion to become God's otherness. Our worship, and so our humanity, gains clearest focus when the sheer gratuity of our being, all being, moves us to prayers such as Ps. 115 ("Not to us, O Lord, not to us, but to your name give glory") and the *Te Deum.*

Thanks, as always, for your support. Blessings on your new year.

Gratefully,
John and Denise

~ 46 ~

O God, God,
   no pain or joy blocks you out.
You are my heart's desire
impure and feckless though I be.
If I could have you once and for all,
I could quit this cruel apprenticeship.
What more have I to learn
than my uselessness without you?
You are the beauty for which I hunger,
the lissome love I would embrace.
You are the light arresting my mind,
the darkness beguiling my heart.
I love you in the little children
and the soft hands of the women best.
You smile in what makes me laugh,
in the mischief lightening my burdens.
Happy, I see Satan falling like lightning
when the dullards get their comeuppance.
I see your way of the cross going on
in the street people's shuffling forward,
the whores' selling their souls for the night.
We are the sorriest of all your species,
nearly removing your image from our hearts.
But you, God, can stop our dying
and move us into your life.

~ 47 ~

When I review the history of salvation,
the mighty deeds you have wrought in our world,
the key times are those when you have loved us
beyond even our large capacity to doubt.
Our Exodus and Sinai,
the formative days of our youth,
drew us forth from doubts about our meaning,
drew us into a partnership with you.
But we lost this innocent intimacy
through distraction and the dust of the world.
We learned not to expect special conversations —
part maturation, part loss of faith.
Slowly we focused on human experience generally,
how you have and have not tended to come.
Now, O God, little surprises us
and little consoles us.
We wonder each day why you allow so much pain.
But we know that you must still find it good
that we do not know —
that still our task is to live with you by faith.
Support us in this living, we pray.
Support all your groping, wounded people.
Remember the weakness of our frame.
And do not let our backs bend to breaking.

~ 48 ~

I watch the clouds move eastward,
beauty blowing stagnation out
as I follow music, art, and prayer
down toward consolation.
Nothing human is foreign to you.
You have made everything good.
Grant us, then, to move on the good —
ride your creatures toward you.
The wine that we drink
should put praise on our tongue,
the bread that we eat
should bow low for your blessing.
The work that we do is work for you.
Who else can justify it?
And what, O God, about our sufferings?
Why should we not end this wretched existence
so full of pain and disappointment?
Only because we feel deep in our spirits
that our lives are not ours to dispense.
You grant us life as you wish
and you take it away when that pleases you.
If we pretend to sovereignty over our time
we worship ourselves as idols.
So give us this day
the strength that we need to keep trying.
Raise up the levee, O God,
and keep all of your people safe.

~ 49 ~

Death terrifies the majority
making them slow and stupid.
They don't want to face the facts
so they pretend I want business as usual.
How can I want business as usual?
What half-wit could really think that?
I want people to walk a middle line
between ignoring my disease and fixating on it.
I want people to make me feel
that they too are mortal,
that what happens to me today
they know will happen to them all too soon.
Too often my healthy friends wax superior
as though the glow on their skin
were a sure sign of election.
It is not so.
You, God, do not judge as mortal creatures do.
You want the sinner to be converted,
want just people who live with pure hearts.
I should pray for all your terrified people.
You have blessed me with time.
For months and months
I have lived with no illusion.
If I am still stupid,
I have only myself to blame.
Treat my friends as well.

~ 50 ~

Next year in Jerusalem
Jews, Christians, and Muslims will gather
to work for a little more progress
in mutual understanding and respect.
Next year in the City of David,
the City of Jesus,
a city of Muhammad,
the children of Abraham will pursue again
the implications of their common monotheism.
O God,
be enough for us.
Let us feel that our plain confession of you
undercuts our centuries of warfare,
all the differences in our religious styles,
all the cultural distances we must travel.
There is only you,
sovereign from heaven.
To you we all bow,
before you we all stand naked.
The keener our sense of you
the better our dialogue will go.
So give us, O God,
your angelic helpers
to keep us on the path that is straight.
Help us all to live by faith
so that nothing passing distracts us.

~ 51 ~

When I go about among your people,
   the pain of so many lays me low.
Physically or mentally
pain seems more the rule than the exception.
Typical faces are lined deep with worry.
I have given up trying to understand.
It makes no sense that the world should run by torment.
I know nothing else to do
but come before you in protest
asking night and day
that you right this wrong,
supplying the peace that I cannot.
We are not gods.
The best of us can alleviate pain only momentarily.
Why, O God, have you made your people for suffering?
Could you not have arranged things better,
protected your children at their games?
Or is pain some strange show of your kindness for us,
a high way to bring us to heaven?
That does not sound right,
but you can see that I am becoming desperate.
My mind does not know where to turn.
At best, I can only wait and watch and wonder.
One day
you will reveal why things are as they are.
One day
all manner of thing may be well.

~ 52 ~

Our bodies are our selves;
   as they break down we do.
Even though with time we may accept this,
it insinuates a soul-deep sadness.
You have made our flesh for flourishing.
We have skin for feeling,
tongues for tasting,
ears for hearing babies laugh.
You did not make us, O God,
for pain and brokenness.
We ought not to hear women weeping.
Do you not resent the ruin of your handiwork?
Are not war and disease your enemies?
I know nothing, God, about how you think.
Your wisdom is too much for me.
I cannot lift it with ideas,
thoughts to excuse you from cruelty.
I cannot flee from the challenge of it,
keep injustice and evil under your heel.
The child visiting her cancerous mother,
the wife watching her husband waste away,
haunt my dreams of the night
and the morning strews locusts and beetles
across the land.
I want, then, for the day of your disclosure,
trying in the meanwhile
to let you do what you feel you must,
trying in very poor patience
to possess at least part of my soul.

LETTER TEN

April 15, 1994

Dear Friends,

Things have been going well on the health front. I have tolerated the second course of chemotherapy (melphalan and dexamethasone) well and the protein marker has stayed around 1.5 (low/good). In March we tested our stamina with a trip to Mexico City: no problems.

The big news is that we are moving to California at the end of August. Denise has accepted a position at Santa Clara University as Hanley Professor and Chair of Religious Studies. Tulsa has been good to us, but after nine years a new opportunity held considerable allure. Santa Clara has a large department, with rich potential, and we have friends in the area of twenty-five years standing, since my years at Stanford. A temporary address from mid-August can be the SCU Religious Studies Department, Santa Clara, CA 95053.

As I turn the corner into what is statistically my last year, I realize how limited such estimates are, yet also how necessary it is not to forget them. Recently, my images for myeloma have taken on a quality of slumbering violence. In the forest primeval, I wait for ocelot grace, listen for the leopard's cough. Many days life is far less taut, my spirit far less collected. But now and then the nothingness regains its edge. In terms of the distinction we owe to Clausewitz, "real war" returns to center stage, chastening thoughts of an ideal "true war." The task is to meet the mystery where it presents itself, not where I might like it to be. The call is to let even torpor serve God's purposes, a lumpen benefaction. Maybe some of this is just resting, getting ready for the leopard's roar. Fortunately, it causes little worry. Absent sharp pain, I'm content to wait. Sometimes the support of your prayers is tangible. Always we think of you gratefully, affectionately.

Of the making of books there seems no end. *Cancer and Faith* (Twenty-Third) has appeared. *In the Path of the Masters* (Paragon) is imminent. *Christianity,* 3d ed. (Wadsworth), and *Your Word Is Near* (Upper Room) are in production. Denise's constructive Christian feminist theology (Blackwell) is inching along, as is our study of mysticism in the world religions (Oxford). It's a blessing to be able to work decently more days than not. It redeems a lot of the time. May you all (Tulsa is southern) be finding the same.

Love,
John and Denise

~ 53 ~

Now thank we all our God
for sunshine and frisky rabbits,
for money in the drawer and the bank,
for the juice to take two and hit to right.
Even in the midst of our pain
sometimes you give pasta and tequila,
moonlight shimmering on the river,
Bach beating beauty in our blood.
I do not want to forget
all the yeses that I should be saying.
I do not want all the nos I must say
to occlude my sight like a wall.
When I have the choice,
grant me a hopeful spirit
an inclination to move forward
a will to consecrate one more day
to trust.
I no longer know what the game is,
see now only the faintest imprint of the rules.
Necessarily, though, two paths diverge,
one of hope and one of suspicion.
Through ages past you have supported me,
never allowed me to sink full under.
So would it not be churlish, God,
for me to stop hoping now?
Would it not be a mortal amnesia to forget
yours are the times, yours are the reasons,
I am only a renter?

~ 54 ~

✦ How good it is to have friends
with whom we can celebrate or lament.
The indifference of the world is half our suffering.
The delight of our friends is half our joy.
You have made us social, God,
in reflection of yourself.
We have arms and legs for coupling.
It is not good for us to be alone.
Sometimes I wish I were alone
because my illness worries others.
Sometimes I wish I could give up,
stop fighting,
hasten the inevitable day
when my marrow is simply too tired;
I can no longer make good blood.
But I cannot give up
for I do not belong to myself.
You, God, hold the paper on me.
My wife has the right that I try to live.
Why, then, do I not trust you more profoundly?
If I am not my own possession,
why do I not rest content with your disposition of me?
If I live it is your doing.
If I die it is your will.
Living or dying
I am nothing but your creature
perhaps, even more, your child.

~ 55 ~

✦ How much of our suffering is a challenge from you?
Do we become more fully human
by dealing with brokenness, enduring failure and loss?
In the desert Israel marched closest to you.
In the Exile pain produced the best poetry.
On the cross Jesus gained a new universality.
Death in his family taught Muhammad compassion.
And I, O God, what have I been learning?
What have the tears of my wife brought home?
Without your grace I have no faith.
Without hope of you my desire to live vanishes.
My body can hammer down my spirit
but my spirit can lift my body up.
My spirit can depress my body
but my body can raise my spirit up.
Well or ill, I am complicated, fragile, changing.
Ill or well, I am only half myself
if not communing with you.
Ill, the world without you is bloody,
an asylum for the insane.
Well, the world without you is silly
flattened down to beer and fun.
For me to be with any beauty
I must be in your midst
living with you and living for you.
In my blood you move all the molecules.
In my bones you squeeze me to cracking.
You squeeze my bones to cracking.
O God, my great love, let pain help me to please you
and let dying send me home.

~ 56 ~

Many of our religious leaders seem stupid.
As much as worldly bureaucrats,
they focus on rules and trivia.
Even their concern for morality is misguided.
People in love with you do not become great sinners.
People shown your incomparable beauty,
the lines by which you draw the honest mind,
the hopes by which you stir the pure of heart,
do what is right connaturally.
Yes, we all remain sinners,
self-centered and dull to the end.
But by the gift of your uncreated Spirit
we applaud the least show of wit or compassion,
the smallest goodness expressing your image.
We want your starlight to take our breath away.
We will watch waves crash against rocks for hours.
Mencius knew that none of us will let a toddler perish.
Any child heading for an open well becomes our own.
Why don't our religious leaders
build on this human nature?
Why don't they see the naturalness of grace?
The world is a cornucopia of sacraments.
Holy interactions occur everywhere,
even Capitol Hill and Wall Street.
A shake of the hands, a kiss on the cheek —
if we had souls with which to see we'd discern you.
The real job of our religious leaders
is to lure us to the mountain air:
Sinai, Zion, Carmel,
Tabor, Golgotha, Fuji.
Less carping and moralizing,
more freedom, mysticism, and love.

LETTER ELEVEN
July 15, 1994

Dear Friends,

It's a busy time, a lot going on. We've been to California and back, driving one of our cars and settling parts of our move to Santa Clara University. We saw the desert in Arizona and received wonderful hospitality both there and in California. Now we are packing and finishing — hard work.

The myeloma has kept coming back, lately invading hip bone and skull. So I've started a new chemotherapy, VAD. It runs through a Groshong catheter in my chest — bionic. The chemicals make a good, heavy hit.

We fly to the East Coast on July 15, return on August 12, and hope to be established in Santa Clara by September 1. You can get our itinerary from the Religion Department, University of Tulsa.

This new chemotherapy and the move suggest that we are entering a new phase of our trek. It's under the same cloud by day, pillar of fire by night, but we see new cactuses. We've finished all our contractual obligations to our publishers. For a while I'll probably hide out. Our physical strength for offering hospitality in California may be limited. Please understand.

The phrase humming in my brain today is, "Quaerens me sedisti lassus." It comes (I think) from the Dies Irae but it carries more peace than wrath. Sitting by the Samaritan well, dusty and spent, Jesus is no hound of heaven. He's just tired. God wears him out, eventually to the fractures of Calvary. So with the rest of us, one way or another, sooner or later. Breakdown is a divine as well as a human way. No disciples are above their master. He sits by the well for us.

Blessings on your summer. It's 100 degrees in Tulsa and climbing. We've begun sailing on Half Moon Bay.

Love,
John and Denise

~ 57 ~

✦ O God, you teach me a new ethic,
stimulated by a new question:
How to treat the terminally ill?
My ten-year-old nephew knows this ethic,
keeping faith with me month after month.
My fifty-year-old friend does not know it,
becoming ever more erratic and inconstant.
Terminal illness means that time is short,
the drama of human vulnerability focuses clearly.
With the terminally ill
we cannot put things off.
Fidelity becomes a high premium.
So I find myself dividing up the month,
marking up my own calendar
so that the people I know who are in trouble
get my regular attention.
One time I send a card,
another time I make a call.
Practiced now in receiving such messages
I know that remembrance is all.
We can't do much for the terminally ill
sometimes practical things — money, cooking, visiting;
more frequently all we can do is care and pray.
The ill know this thoroughly
as they know that they are always alone.
But sometimes care can tame loneliness,
milk much of its poison away.
So not to care faithfully, regularly, dependably
is not to be a significant friend.

~ 58 ~

Winter knocks in the early morning,
begging for a little heat to take off the chill.
Your natural world keeps on turning
oblivious to our human crises.
In the war zones people look down another tunnel —
seeing more cold, deprivation, starvation.
The madness of war, of ethnic cleansing,
of agreeing to starve even children
makes us human beings unworthy of nature
a mistake thrown into a world otherwise without hate.
No one has solved this horrible problem.
We have had a fully human consciousness
for a hundred thousand years
but we still don't know why
we are divided, marred, sinful.
Each generation has to master its passions anew.
None has done this admirably, adequately,
leaving the rest a model.
Yes, pain offers help, one of its few benefits.
True, over time much that used to drive us,
seduce us, corrupt us,
falls away, rendered irrelevant by pain.
So the man obsessed with possessions looks foolish.
The woman fixated on clothes seems sick.
Life narrows down, simplifies, becomes manageable.
Sufficient for the day is the evil thereof.
The only thing necessary is your love.
If you hold us in the midst of our pains,
we can bear them gracefully.
Now and then we can even thank you
for the enormity that we have to die.

~ 59 ~

✦ Grant us, good God, the faith
    to reconcile ourselves to our dying
and accept the imperfections in our bodies
in the natural world,
in our minds and hearts and souls.
Grant us, even, a proper reconciliation to evil,
our implacable, enduring foe.
After the fact
it "had" to be that Israel suffer through exile,
the Christ gain his glory by crucifixion,
cancer or Alzheimer's disease or heart attack
twist our cells and lives.
We understand none of the reasons for this.
If we were God the world would be perfect.
But you are God,
and the world is not perfect
so we have to wait upon your revelation.
As God, you are perfect.
An imperfect God is a contradiction,
a gross intellectual blunder.
Can you be perfect in, through, and above evil?
Can your deathlessness redeem our dying and pain
in the new creation that believers call heaven?
We wait in terrible longing,
begging your help to hang on,
praying to serve what we cannot see,
but know that we still may love.

LETTER TWELVE

October 15, 1994

Dear Friends,

We spent four weeks in Connecticut and Massachusetts, mid-July to mid-August, seeing family and friends in Boston, and then relaxing at the beach in Gloucester. Having returned to Tulsa for two weeks, we flew to San Jose on August 27. August 29 we moved into the little house that we are renting. Denise took over as Chair of Religious Studies at Santa Clara September 1, and since then we have been calling ourselves Californians. The weather has cooperated — skies of striking beauty — and Denise has been making good progress getting her new job under control. Be on the lookout for the reprints of the Santa Clara Lecture Series, which begins at the end of October with a talk by John Meier.

On the health front, complicated news: two sessions of the VAD regime for which I had the Groshong catheter inserted June 23 did nothing against the myeloma. While in Boston we arranged a consultation at Dana Farber cancer hospital. There the recommendation was a regime of high-dose cytoxan and investigating peripheral stem cell transplantation. Two weeks or so after we arrived here I was so short of breath (hemoglobin 7, about half of normal) that I got four units of blood. Two weeks after that I had the first (seven-hour) infusion of the cytoxan, which gave me no problems for a week. Then I developed an infection in the catheter and ended up in the hospital for a week, getting antibiotics, new blood, and platelets, and having the infected catheter removed. The problem was battling an infection at a time when my blood

103

counts were very low (white counts .5, less than 100 for the neutrophils, platelets down to 14,000 at one point — wimpy blood indeed: about 10 percent of normal). Anyway, all ended well, but we got a dramatic lesson in the tolls the chemotherapy has taken over the past two and a half years, as well as in the dangers of the new, quite toxic regimen.

No great revelations came during my recent week in the hospital. It was sobering to be again on a floor reserved for patients with cancer (or AIDS). My fellow patients were reacting variously: mania, depression, a wan smile. I was the only one among perhaps forty who closed my door regularly (I had a laptop computer and pounded out a chapter). The others seemed to want to keep a port open to the normal world — touching.

We all want to be normal, healthy, full of energy and prospects. It is hard to accept, again and again, that a central part of human normalcy is being mortal, fragile, increasingly likely to break down. Recently I saw pictures taken right after a friend and I had run a marathon in Wichita. It seemed a scene from another life. Still, I assure you, this remains a good life. More days than not we hear grace notes, and regularly we experience liberations — so many things I no longer have to care about. Now and then pain even enhances our prayer.

Blessings on all of you whose support we feel often, and who we hope share in whatever benefits this strange, cruciform time may generate. As I walked around the cancer ward, I sensed a drama in the omnipresent suffering. Something was assembling itself — I hope a glory eye has not seen. From the old people no longer rational to the young people laid low by AIDS, the whole group deserved to be taken under the shelter of angels' wings, given finally their condign rest. It was easy to ask God that they would be, with every tear wiped from their eyes.

Love,
John and Denise

~ 60 ~

Help us, O God, to want your will done in us,
cheerfully, joyfully, generously.
Let us see that we have no better word than "amen,"
no higher function or fuller dignity.
Help us to accept without fuss
whatever you ask of us
especially when it is so banal and obvious
as suffering poor health,
giving up prideful ambition,
walking along the way of the cross.
The way of the cross is the way of the world
though the world
both around me and in me
does not know it and hates it.
But who does not finally suffer,
break down and come apart at the seams?
Who does not have to accept
failure, disappointment, dying?
have to contend with failure, disappointment, death?
Perhaps only those who strip themselves
or let you strip them
so that they want nothing but what you want,
so that whether they live or die,
succeed or fail,
is indifferent
because everything except you is insignificant,
means nothing if not in you and for you.
I have no strength to strip myself like this.
If you want it, God, you must do it yourself
and I pray that you do it gently.

~ 61 ~

✦ You can be doing good in me,
running the whole world around me
regardless of what I think.
You can be making me into what you wish
regardless of whether I am aware of this,
almost regardless of whether I want it.
For you are nearly everything
and I am nearly nothing.
The margins separating you from everything
and me from nothing
are paper thin.
I am as little separate from you,
as little independent of you,
as I can be and still have a self,
still be not divine, just another cracked little creature.
Yet I am also so far from you
that I have no understanding of you
except what you give me,
most beautifully in passing touches
well below images or ideas.
O God, make all this soft language
no mere reflection on being —
how my *is* flows from your totality.
Make it, I pray,
completely personal between us,
the losses and gains of fey lovers,
the coin to pay Christian Charon
to row my broken boat away.

~ 62 ~

The refinements of love are endless
but for the dying perhaps finally simple.
In your Spirit
we can just let go.
We do not have to care how we look
even in your sight.
It can be enough to want to survive
if and as you desire.
We are the work of your hands,
smeared and bleared by sin
but always more your doing
than any of our own.
You know what you have made
and we pray that you do not regret it.
You move in wisdom
and what you make establishes beauty.
You hold all priority, all judgment,
and most responsibility.
Why then do we nations rage?
What self-importance keeps us spinning?
Should we not rather let go,
give in, attend, abide?
From shore to shore the waves worship you
assembling themselves without fuss.
If your Spirit moves they grow lively.
If your Spirit stays they grow calm.
Attune us to your Spirit.

LETTER THIRTEEN
January 17, 1995

Dear Friends,

The rains have left us soggy but still happy to be here. Denise is learning the intricacies of scheduling the teaching of thirty people and preparing to deliver the second of the new Santa Clara Lectures (let us know if you did not get the first, by John Meier, on the miracles of Jesus). Since the University of Tulsa has closed down the Warren Lectures, this new series can slip into a well-established niche. On the book front, my *Psalms for Times of Trouble* has just appeared from Twenty-Third, and we expect four books to appear in the fall (two from Oxford, one from Blackwell, and one from Trinity).

I have been profiting from a different regime of chemotherapy high-dose (40 mg/kg) cytoxan. Three administrations have reduced the paraprotein marker (which had climbed to a worrisome 6.2) more than 50 percent, and I am recovering now from a fourth. There is only a small, adjuvant dose of steroid (dexamethasone) accompanying each eight-hour administration, so I have been moving back to a normal metabolism, taste, and weight. The cytoxan steals hair, leaving only a little down, and this has led me to acquire a small array of felt hats. I have a gray Akubra, in homage to Down Under, a gray dress Stetson with a jaunty feather, and a chocolate working cowboy's hat. Sometimes I see these hats as more than just ways to warm a bald head. Sometimes they strike me as signs of life, like the petunia on the sill of the ghetto window.

What lessons from our God? Ah, strange mystery. We have

been working on Ruth and Jonah (*lectio divina*), so providence and the largess of God have been the scriptural filters. The cytoxan has effected a reprieve, probably temporary, but a reminder nonetheless that it is not for any of us to say what can happen, what cannot change. It is for us to try to live at the edge, the scalpel line, where God moves the present into the future. The man Jesus did not know the future into which his preaching or dying was moving him. No human being can. There is nothing new under the sun, and yet there is also a new creation, of which he became the first-born. So we watch, and we pray, and we trust — imperfectly indeed, but still passionately, full of good fire and happy determination.

Blessings on your winter.

Love,
John and Denise

~ 63 ~

Give me the strength to call myself "untroubled."
Help me to let go of my grievances and worries.
I want to be more than my pains.
I ought to be greater than my frustrations.
In the sunshine, walking through the park,
I feel that I am indeed greater.
Though the grass withers and the flowers fade
they intimate an unconquerable whole.
The least terns fly in on schedule
and it matters less that I am dying.
This can happen in any direction.
You can take me out to the fields and streams
or down through the layers of consciousness
or in toward the shard of my core being.
Every direction stops my mouth.
Only you make the world.
The postmodern blather about our making the world
is but rouge on a dead intellect.
So I stretch my arms in every direction,
fill my lungs and root my feet
to take part humbly for a moment,
no more significant than the bulldog
ambling over to water the tree.
The stink of the river rises,
suggesting that sin too takes part,
but only for a moment, and then all the air clears.

~ 64 ~

The moment of crisis comes
when we realize that there is no answer to discover;
the only way to go forward
is to keep on suffering through.
We want the peoples to praise you in their crises
for you have made them a beautiful world,
but we see that the peoples mainly
praise not you but themselves,
Xenophon's dogs worshiping gods that look like dogs.
And I, O God,
whom do I praise and worship?
In a dark night,
my soul at rest,
I sometimes think I have come home,
but there is no home in thinking.
Only your Spirit lets us abide.
It is good, though, to laugh at this crisis,
see the folly in our mind's coming apart.
There will be coffee again tomorrow.
Shall I eat a donut with it or an apple?
When the mind goes on chemical walkabout,
simple things become precious tethers.
So I thank you for the pain in my knees
and the itch of my reddening skin,
even the sprint of my steroidal brain.
They hold me here,
pacify my spirit,
and just maybe bring me your touch.

~ 65 ~

✦ Hard pain takes away reason,
transforming our prayer to passion.
When the body is racked,
we can do nothing that feels lovely.
You have chosen to tear us apart,
slashing the flesh you once formed.
In the mysterious ways of your so savage love
you have become a consuming fire,
a cancer holocausting our bones.
There is nothing genteel in real suffering,
no Calvin Klein blusher or premium cologne.
Real suffering is raw, shocking, horrible,
knocking "success" into a crumbled cocked hat.
Chemicals taint my taste
as sin taints my memory.
Nothing is pure or dependable.
All my awareness is slanted.
So you must be my awareness,
the reality of a faith below taint.
When I let go, stop thinking,
enter the pain as though it were your arms,
I come close to dissolving in your reality.
Let it be that this leads to a new creation,
praise in song for your full glory,
endless gazing upon your pure beauty,
no let or hindrance or cease.

~ 66 ~

✦ The step of the old woman becomes feeble
and she lets her thoughts turn toward death.
She has exceeded the biblical span,
watched four score of years come and go.
Aging is a rich trouble.
What we learn exceeds what we suffer.
For everything there is a time.
We grope for its purpose under heaven.
I am not likely to reach the biblical span.
I shall hold back the onward march of longevity.
It does not matter, and yet of course it does.
We all die ignorant, so it does not matter when.
But the more we have experienced,
the richer our ignorance tends to be.
You are not now the same cloud you were
when Israel departed from Egypt.
You have moved in history, enlarged your story,
and you move in each of our souls.
We never do not know — but this can be ever richer.
At seventy the darkness is more pregnant
than it could be at thirty-five.
"No sé qué," John of the Cross keeps chanting:
"I don't know what."
The simpler our sense of you, the better.
Blank faith is usually more desirable
than visions or prophecies.

~ 67 ~

O God, increase the times when you show us your plan.
If we can hope that our pain serves a purpose —
even just your inscrutable demand that we suffer —
it is less likely to destroy our spirits.
Such a hope tends to come through endurance
building itself up day by day
as we learn that trouble, frustration, and pain
need not be our entire definition.
If often they defeat us,
laying our bodies and minds and spirits low,
sometimes we can resist them,
laugh and celebrate a rainbow.
After the flood Noah enjoyed the rainbow.
It remains a symbol of your pledge
never again to destroy the world by water.
The rainbows in personal experience,
the times of beauty and peace after the deluge,
can be equally symbolic.
So once I watched a woman
come out of her treatment,
then square her shoulders and grin at her daughter:
"Let's get a burger and a beer!"
You had moved in her spirit, stirred up her feistiness,
and given her back her self.
When her pain had gotten in all its licks,
she discovered that she was still standing,
and that she was still more than her woe.

~ 68 ~

Let the enemies of my friends be your enemies.
Let those who make life hard for your people perish.
Yes, God, we need forgiving hearts.
Put them in our breasts, flesh instead of stone.
But do move in our world against the wicked.
Do ride out at the front of the poor,
a mighty warrior this day as always.
Most of our suffering is unnecessary,
less the product of your evolutionary plan
than the result of our own stupidity and sin.
We will not share your creation fairly.
We will not live as brothers and sisters,
equally mortal and equally blessed.
Punish us, O God, to our reformation.
Let the pain of our disorders instruct us.
If only when we have aged,
let us know that life could have been different.
Faith and hope and love would have transformed us.
I believe in your darkness; help you my unbelief.
I trust in your future; alleviate you my fear.
I love you; make my love unconditional.
You yourself must work these transformations.
My becoming spirit of your Spirit is your doing.
But today I can feel that you are with me,
so today what does not seem possible?
If you wish you can raise the dead.

LETTER FOURTEEN
April 15, 1995

Dear Friends,

The weather has been excellent lately, giving us clear views of emerald hills and stunning flowers. It is a good time for Easter to arrive. We have renewed our pledge to get to the ocean once a week, usually to San Francisco or Monterey. The success of my current regime of chemotherapy has allowed me to do this with zest, and even to return to serious swimming (a mile every other day). The index for the mass of tumor has fallen almost two-thirds since I began the high-dose cytoxan in September. It is now three years since my diagnosis — the mean time of survival. Although the nearly full-time chemotherapy (only four months off in three years) has taken its toll, the index is now below half of what it was when I was diagnosed in 1992. Your prayers, and a lot of fine medical treatment, have worked wonders. Denise and I still have to move our horizon along month by month, guided by the numbers, and the long-term prospects have not changed. Indeed, it is not clear whether any reasonable treatments remain, after this regime of cytoxan loses its punch. But sufficient for this day, in this paschal time, is a great prayer of gratitude.

You know that Christian memory ought to take its shape from the pasch of Jesus. You know that the death and resurrection of the Christ is the axis of our time. Do you know how to accept your constant forgetting of this, and so loss of yourself in distraction, nervousness, boredom, fear, and the bootless rest? Tell me if you do, for I have yet to secure it, though I have made a little progress in not worrying about being so slow. Regardless of what we do, fortunately, Jesus works and dies and is raised by his Father. Thereby, nothing changes, yet everything does. We work and die and hope for resurrection. Because of this hope, we can sometimes think that we feel the lift of God's Spirit, the undertow or inertia of grace, holding and moving us. It can become ordinary to be carried through sunrise and sunset toward the verge of resurrection.

Death is the verge of resurrection. At the end of the Creed, the last articles are beautifully hopeful: the communion of saints, the forgiveness of sins, the resurrection of the body, and the life of the world to come. When these words have become like the rocks of the Zen teaching story, as ordinary after enlightenment as they were before, yet completely different, we can think that the Spirit of God is no illusion, rather the senior partner in the whole enterprise of our pilgrimage, the whole making of our self. Grateful blessings on your own paschaltide.

Love,
John and Denise

~ 69 ~

All life moves through dying.
My illness can teach me that.
If we want to progress toward you,
we have to leave old gods far behind.
You are our absolute future,
the beckoning whither of our now.
You call us out of slavery,
away from the onions and leeks,
onward and upward toward your freedom,
which we enter by saying yes to we know not what.
The only check on our squatting down in unbelief
is the blank one of abandoning ourselves to you.
The only way the saints find worth walking
is giving up their will for your own.
You parcel your will out day by day,
asking us to wait upon it patiently.
You take over our spirits and bones through our aging,
preparing the dissolution of our old selves,
necessary if we are to share your own nature.
O God, you are our most intimate happening;
the drama of our lives is your script.
Not a hair falls from our heads,
not a pain moves through our limbs,
except by your choice and provision.

~ 70 ~

✦ Help us, O God, to remember to pray
for all your people who forget to,
the troubled, busy, confused swarm
who do not know where to send their hearts.
They want and need and long
but for what they never get clear.
They imagine money and pleasure and things,
but their significant wanting comes from their souls,
far below their imaginations.
They want, we all want, nothing less than you yourself.
You have made us for yourself
and our hearts are restless till they rest in you.
The burden and blessing of our human condition
is that we can find fulfillment only beyond
in your so non-human divinity.
Without you, we are but useless passions,
bundles of desire bound to be frustrated.
But with you, we can experience a peace
that the world does not know,
indeed that surpasses our own understanding.
Sometimes, O God, you feel close,
and this lets me think you are always in us.
I thank you now for those times
and I pray that you give them to all your people.

~ 71 ~

✦ I do not control your Spirit,
   so I cannot control my dying.
Whenever I feel separated from your Spirit,
I lie as though unredeemed in a pit.
Animal vitality is passing.
Remarkable, cause for praise, always it finally crashes.
Spiritual vitality requires crashing,
your breaking us apart,
our finally realizing we cannot understand you;
we have always to journey by faith.
In the darkness of that journey,
the pain and fear and doom,
we learn that you will be what you choose to show us,
that you will speak your name only night by night.
O God, help me listen for your speaking.
Give me the ear of a lover,
the collectedness of a disciple.
Help me to abide,
not squiggle and squirm away.
When I run from my death, it nips at my heels.
When I abide, it backs away.
Yes, you are my final passion,
the awfulness of all your otherness.
But you are also my bliss
and my freedom from all lesser harassments.
Be you then also, God,
my good death and everlasting life.

~ 72 ~

✦ By making us suffer
   you teach us who you are not.
You are not our mommy or daddy.
You are not our saccharine friend.
You are only yourself,
and I am a fool until I accept this.
All idolaters are fools.
The beginning of wisdom is fear of the Lord.
We do not fear our idols.
We love them and caress them because they please us.
You do not please us.
You only please yourself.
If we praise your pleasing yourself,
join the great chorus of lower creation,
we can come into the exquisite pleasure
of being exactly what we ought to be:
worshipers of your overwhelming splendor.
But this fulfills our being, meets our nature,
while having little to do with superficial pleasure.
There is no ego in right worship.
There is no concern for getting our own back
or oiling ourselves with satisfaction.
Worship is direct adoration of you
the rush of our spirits and hearts and minds,
with no detours toward self-satisfaction,
with complete delight in your being our All.

LETTER FIFTEEN
July 15, 1995

Dear Family,

A week ago we thought that this would probably be the last generic letter. Since May the myeloma has gotten the better of the chemotherapy, doubling the amount of cancer. We had run out of tested therapies (the high-dose cytoxan that had worked well since September itself was a stretch), and so we were stymied. However, three days ago my oncologist here spoke with the researcher at Dana Farber with whom we had consulted last summer and came away with an idea worth trying. It involves using VP16, a regime proven effective in several cancers but little tested for myeloma. Indeed, there is nothing published on its use for myeloma. However, the researcher, Robert Schlossman, M.D., knew of some inchoate work, and my oncologist here, Klaus Porzig, M.D., has had good success with VP16 in other cancers. So as soon as we can get my blood strong enough to try it (the myeloma has started to wreck my red cells), we'll give it a go.

We found out about the return of the myeloma after a good week on the East Coast in June. There we went to the Catholic Theological Society of America's annual meeting (New York this year), where, in a moment golden for us, we received the CTSA's John Courtney Murray award (the first couple to receive it in the fifty-year history). It was an added treat that members of both our families and two sets of friends could be present. Then it was on to Washington to meet with more friends and see some great art. We ended in Baltimore with a lovely visit with Denise's family. Quite a week. Since our return Northern California has been putting on a spectacular show of good weather. Some days at the ocean the beauty makes you clap your hands in pure thanks.

It's a roller-coaster life, as perhaps all lives are. The invitation has been to live fully, gratefully, while practicing the art of dying. You will remember that learning to die is one of Plato's descriptions of philosophy, the love of wisdom. You will also remember that the Johannine Jesus, our current study project, works signs and dies to offer us eternal life. Dying/living. Learning to die while loving living. Realizing that an incarnate divinity knows this biphased rhythm of human existence from within. Trying therefore to become, not callous about pain or death, nor presumptuous, but free of their power to loom up as frightening idols and block out the far greater reality of God. Any of our lives is a small thing. Measured by the calipers of astrophysical evolution, it does not stretch for a micro-inch. And yet each of our lives stands before God, comes directly from God, utterly clear in its specificity, for God, having no limits, is not overcome by the swarm of us creatures but in the divine patience out of time can love each of us just for ourselves. So we wait, letting our aging, sickening bodies instruct us as much as our minds, and remembering that we have not been called servants but friends.

Love,
John and Denise

~ 73 ~

Run fast-forward by drugs,
I babble before you
wondering with considerable humor
whether I can rely on anything I feel.
The same with anything I think:
what is the worth of thoughts sprung
from an abnormal bodily chemistry?
O God, we rely on ordinariness,
on health and consistency,
to give us a dependable world.
But you are not ordinary.
Your light spills outside the span we can see.
Your palette is richer than our rainbow.
And you are present in all our ways of being,
both the ordinary and the unusual,
both the healthy and the ill.
Nothing defeats you, God.
If my brain breaks
you are still wise
and your wisdom can still save me.
If I lose my hope because of pain,
you do not cease being the ground
of a hope fully realistic.
Warm these stark stones, God, I pray.
Help me to feel in them your care.
Death is an objective dissolution.
Make it a personal passover into your dazzling love.

~ 74 ~

✦ You give us two commands
and let them merge into one.
We are to love you with all our hearts
and to love our neighbors as ourselves.
More simply, we are to love always and everywhere:
our friends and our enemies,
the skies above and the earth under our feet.
For you are love,
and those who abide in love abide in you.
It could not be plainer, more sharply focused:
the greatest of your gifts is love;
love is our only crucial obligation.
I love you, God, and have for all my adult life.
I love you badly, distractedly, impurely,
but from first I knew what your name meant,
first received the slightest inkling,
I knew you were all I needed or wanted
and my life gained purpose and order.
What shall I return to you
for all the favors that loving you has brought me?
I shall dwell in the thought of you,
the hope for you,
the trust in your care for me,
and the love that you pour forth in my heart
all the days of my life
and all your heaven to come.

~ 75 ~

✦ O God, at the end of the day, the life, the book,
you should increase and we should decrease.
We should be but dust and ashes;
you should be all in all.
If the world makes any sense,
if our lives have any meaning,
if our sins do not x us out as failures,
it is because you are all that is crucial.
We die and fade from significance
unless you live and take us to yourself.
We sin and are stained with guilt
unless you are holy and forgive us.
Nothing in the world is essentially different from us.
All the rest of creation is finite or mortal;
all the rest of humanity is sinful and guilty.
Either there is you, the creator wholly uncreated,
or there is chaos, irrationality, frustration,
and so no explanation for the facts of the world.
Dear God, do not let us suffer without explanation.
Be God so clearly, stand by us so palpably,
that our sufferings fall into perspective.
If our great passion is only the praise of your glory
so that we really pray that your will be done,
nothing can separate us from your love,
no crucifixion place us apart from your grace.
So send forth, O God, your Spirit,
and hear our halfling psalms.

John Tully Carmody died September 23, 1995.
May light perpetual shine upon him,
and may his words comfort and inspire us
as we face our own mortality.